OUTHOUSES

Along the White Oak

OUTHOUSES

Along the White Oak

Jack Dudley

ISBN 0-9678787-0-5

Printed in China

Coastal Heritage Series, 409 N. 35th Street, Morehead City, NC 28557
Jack Dudley, Author

Introduction

In 1976, the USA celebrated its 200th anniversary. Almost every community heralded the Bicentennial year with some form of celebration, raising America's historical awareness to an all–time high. These celebrations enhanced my historical interest, getting me going on what has become a decades–long avocation, documenting North Carolina's coastal history and fokelore through the eye of a camera. In just a few years, I photographed many artifacts, examples of folk art and historical structures. I also copied hundreds of old photographs.

The old photographs quickly became the focus of my interests. Old pictures portray a vivid account of life of yesteryear. In the backgrounds of numerous photographs were barely discernable little structures that today we call outhouses. In the old days, most people referred to them simply as toilets. The outhouses were an unrecognized part of the landscape, yet such an integral part of an earlier era. They now have become a part of America's vanishing past.

These small architectural gems triggered my interest in exploring the countryside adjoining the White Oak River. Quite a few outhouses still stood 20 years ago, but most were abandoned, many overgrown with vines or dwarfed with weeds and saplings. Over 40 outhouses were documented by old photographs or in new photographs showing structures shrouded by greenery.

Over two decades later, I attempted to retrace my footsteps on the once–trodden paths to the necessary houses. All but one had vanished! Time stands still for few of our earthly possessions. Outhouses are truly part of America's vanishing architecture.

The White Oak River

The White Oak River, forming a part of the boundaries of Onslow, Carteret and Jones Counties, appears on the earliest maps of North Carolina as the Weetock River. The Indians of the area, part of the Algonkian Nation, gave the river its name. Archaeological digs have revealed many characteristics of the Native Americans, including those who lived in villages that had palisaded walls and refuse pits. In all probability the Indians who lived in villages had primitive pit privies where they performed their scatological rites.

In the early 1700s, the White Oak River was opened for settlement through land grants, and people began to enter the region. In time, a number of large and productive plantations lined the White Oak shores. During the Colonial through Antebellum Periods, the White Oak River became a center of naval stores production, and a bustling trade developed with the outside world. During these early years, exports along the river also included significant amounts of lumber, seafood, hides, salt and cotton.

The river served as a highway linking the region to the outside world, first by tall sailing ships and later by power boats. All roads in the area were merely cartpaths, some the forerunners of today's modern roads and highways. Life and prosperity have seen ups and downs, since the Civil War devastated the maritime commerce and regional economy. After the painful recovery of Reconstruction, there was considerable growth and prosperity along the White Oak. Good times continued through the first two decades of the present century until the region became a victim of the Great Depression, yet quite a few buildings and stately homes still stand as architectural reminders of the prosperity of earlier years.

The people who were of the wealthier merchant and planter class were replaced by a humble breed of mariners, fishermen, timber-cutters and small farmers. Basically, everyone derived their livelihood from the land or water.

By the 1950s, the White Oak River area had surrendered most of its isolation and quaintness to an unprecedented population growth and the dubious advantages of modernity, indoor plumbing and the passing of the backhouse.

Remembering the Outhouse

In the past, life was much simpler; people lived off the land and in harmony with Mother Nature. We should revisit the past and reconnect with nature and the simple ways that were once so commonplace. Revisiting the outhouse makes that connection. Despite the influence of modern conveniences and contemporary times, the outhouse is still part of our heritage, and for some it is still a part of everyday life.

Remembering the outhouses gives us a closeness to the soil, an awareness of nature and a reverence for our forefathers and their traditions. Mother Earth reclaims all living things, and nature and the soil all become oneness . Nature never lets us forget our humble beginnings and the fragility of life.

Back in the days when we all used outhouses, no one seemed to notice them. They were simply a necessity of everyday life. With the advent of indoor plumbing, their obsolescence and subsequent neglect have caused their demise. It is a sad but true story, everything in this world must someday meet its end.

In the rural South, most people referred to the outhouse simply as the toilet. Other names around the country are john, jake, biffie, dooley, backhouse, the necessary, the can, and in Australia it is called the dunny. Privy is also a very common name, and it stems from the Latin word privatus denoting privacy.

The preservation and documentation of outhouses is a significant part of our architectural heritage. They are as American as hot dogs and apple pie. They have a simple innocence about them. Graffiti or four letter words were never seen scrawled on the walls of the outhouse.

They should also be remembered as a sanctum where man did some of his best thinking. When we enter the outhouse, it is the one place on earth where mankind and womankind are equal. It does not matter whether we are black or white, rich or poor, male or female, for we are all humbled to the same degree. It is not a case of mind over matter but one of universal matter over mind. When nature calls, there is no ignoring it.

The outhouses have stood in a stately manner for years and served their patrons well; now they belong to another era. Though they are consigned to the past, they have become a part of nature's landscape and a symbol of man's artistry. Outhouses are a part of Americana that touch a soft spot in everyone's heart. The outhouses are fading and fading fast, yet a few still stand along our back roads and byways as silent sentinels to our past, nature's call and life's simpler ways.

Types of Outhouses

Pit Privy

The pit privy was the most popular type of outhouse from the 1930s through the 1950s. One can still obtain a license from local health boards to construct a pit privy. They are reasonably sanitary as long as flies are not attracted and if they are not near a spring or other underground water source. They are not suitable in low, wet areas or in areas that have subterranean rock.

Box & Can Privy

The box and can privy was popular in urbanized areas and was considered a sanitary privy. The workers who dumped the cans were known as scavengers, honey dippers or moonlighters, and the deposits were known as night soil. The night soil was hauled away in a honey wagon and was probably dumped into a river or some other place causing considerable contamination.

Surface Privy

The surface privy was an abominable design, for the excrement lay on the surface making it accessible to chickens, flies and water sources, thus spreading filth and disease. After rain, the contamination washed into water sources, yards, and nearby gardens and fields. It is no surprise that in 1919 a North Carolina State Board of Health study confirmed that human excrement caused 2,000 deaths and 34,000 cases of sickness. Deaths as verified by the State Board of Health statistics were as follows: typhoid...502, dysentery...604, diarrheal diseases of children...875. In the 1920s and 1930s the North Carolina State Board of Health instituted a massive campaign to eliminate the surface privy and replace it with the more sanitary pit privy.

Over-Water Privy

The over-water privy may appear as a joke or cartoon, but it did exist and was very commonplace along the water's edge. The fecal related diseases became waterborne, and it is remarkable that even more deaths did not occur from this nefarious structure.

Architectural Designs

Vaulted-Ceiling

The gabled-roof, also known as the pitched-roof or vaulted-ceiling style, was the most aesthetically pleasing type of outhouse architecture. It was stately in appearance and appeared to be just another outbuilding erected out back. One design merit is that if the roof extended far enough over the door, the door did not tend to warp. The eaves, or overhangs, simply served as a drip cap or stoop. This design was more expensive and difficult to build, and they were considered a luxury only affordable by the well-to-do townspeople and planters.

Saltbox

The saltbox design was quite attractive and functional. The design incorporates a stoop or drip cap over the door. Saltboxes were seen only in the Northeast.

Flat-Top

The flat-top was the simplest to build, but flat roofs inevitably leak. It took builders and architects many years to realize this, for many homes in the 50s and commercial buildings in the 70s were constructed with flat roofs.

Lean-To

The shed-roof or lean-to was by far the most common type of outhouse in the rural South. It was easy to construct, very practical and functional in design and relatively affordable. A disadvantage versus the vaulted ceiling design, is that the door has no overhang to protect it from warping. Wooden doors (yesterday's and today's design) inevitably swell and warp after exposure to the elements. However, lean-tos with tin doors posed no problem with swelling, warping and closure difficulty. An architectural pearl as noted by outhouse humorist Chic Sale* is that the door can be extended to a maximum height, since it will never bump into the roof, regardless of how wide it is opened. Another disadvantage was that the design was the telltale sign of an outhouse. Everyone knew what it was. After the advent of indoor plumbing, many were considered a source of embarrassment and were razed.

*Chic Sale wrote an outhouse book titled **The Specialist**, 1929.

Hip-Roof

The hip-roof style had no architectural advantages. It may have been a more aesthetic design than the lean-to, since it does not have a primitive, earthy appearance. The hip-roof design was seen on military posts and in more sophisticated regions of the country.

Ventilators

Square

The square vent, also dubbed the gunport, is not a well designed vent. In order for it to be functional, it has to be relatively large, and that exposes the interior to stormy weather. When the occupant makes a morning call after a stormy night, he may wake up to a cold, damp seat. It also gives the occupant disconcerting feelings, for the vent is merely a peephole for outside intruders or pranksters.

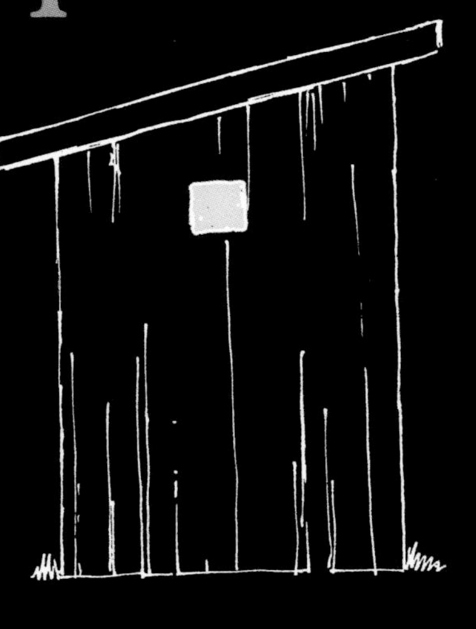

Triangle

The triangle vent is the simplest to incorporate into the lean-to design, yet its large size overexposes the interior to the elements.

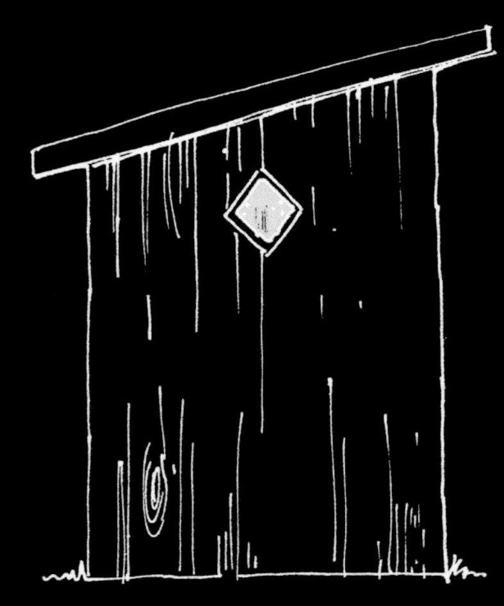

Diamond

The diamond vent is not a well designed vent, for as with the square vent, in order to make it functional, it overexposes the interior to the elements and also becomes a peephole.

The above little symbols are usually designated as ventilators, but that's an ill conceived conclusion since the cutouts are hardly large enough to serve in any functional manner. The crescent or quarter-moon is usually seen in all outhouse cartoons and is regarded as the telltale insignia of an outhouse. Yet I have never seen an authentic crescent in the door of a vintage Carolina outhouse. Large crescents are seen in the doors of many contemporary outhouses, particularly in western regions. According to legend and folklore, the above insignias were seen in facilities

WOMEN

along the stagecoach routes of Pennsylvania and the Northeast in the 1800s. Since the beginning of recorded history, the sun has been a symbol for masculinity, and the moon a symbol for femininity. The star signified sol or solar and was the insignia for the men's outhouse. The moon was the symbol for lunar and was the insignia for the women's outhouse. The star has almost been forgotten, yet the crescent moon lives on as a symbol recognized by everyone.

The louvered vent gives the occupant privacy and is a well designed, functional vent. The only disadvantage is it is more complicated to construct.

Column

The columnar or stack vent is very functional and well designed, for it begins under the privy seat and exits through the roof, thus minimizing foul odors. It was the design recommended by the N. C. State Board of Health.

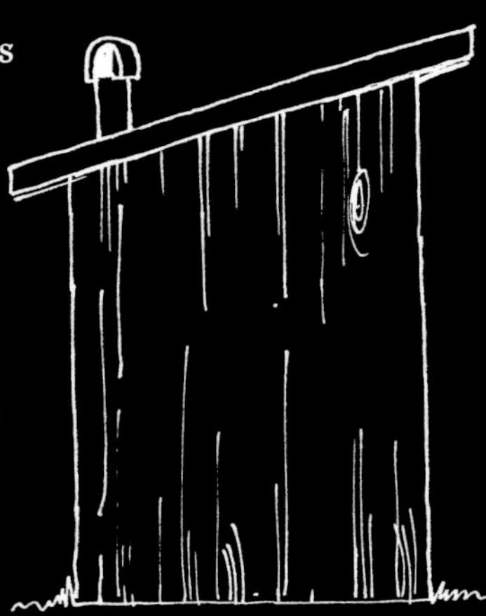

Diagonal

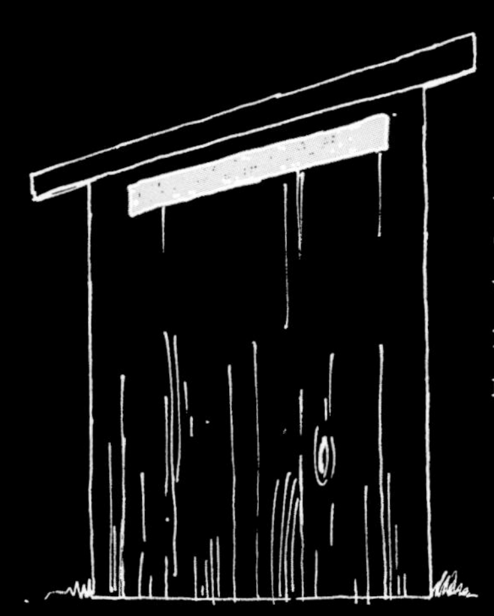

The diagonal or slit vent is a well designed vent, for it is very functional. Also, it is tucked under the eaves of the roof and prevents water from entering the outhouse during windy, rainy weather.

Seat Types

Box

The box seat is simple in design and self explanatory. Some outhouses would have two or more individual boxes (one hole per box). An outhouse with two or more boxes psychologically gives the occupants more space.

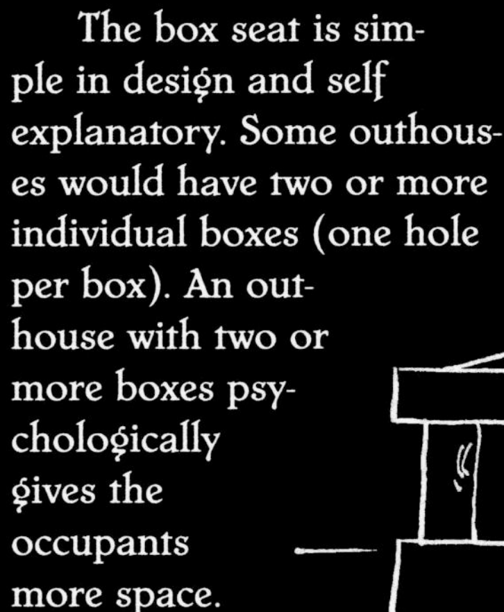

Precast Concrete

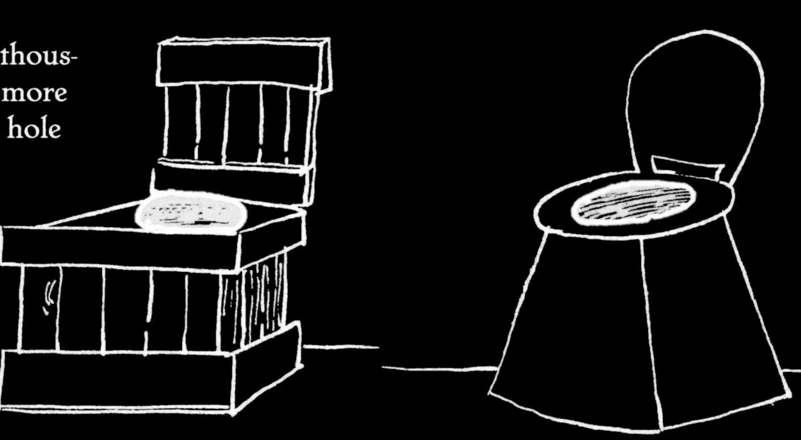

The precast concrete seat looks like a pyramid with the top cropped and capped with a seat. The proper solid geometry term for this design is frustum or truncated tetrahedron. Some were constructed with wooden seats and trap door hole covers, and some had commercially made seats. During the Great Depression, WPA workers produced cast concrete risers and installed them by the hundreds.

Bench

The bench seat was the most popular, and it extended to both side walls. It could have multiple holes with a variety of geometric designs. Some neophytes erroneously called this design a two-seater, not so...this is a two-holer. There were also three-holers, four-holers and so forth.

Store-Bought

The Commercial fixture or closet was a rarity in the countryside, yet Mott Ironworks in New York produced plumbing fixtures by the trainload. Most were for indoor facilities with running water.

Hole Designs

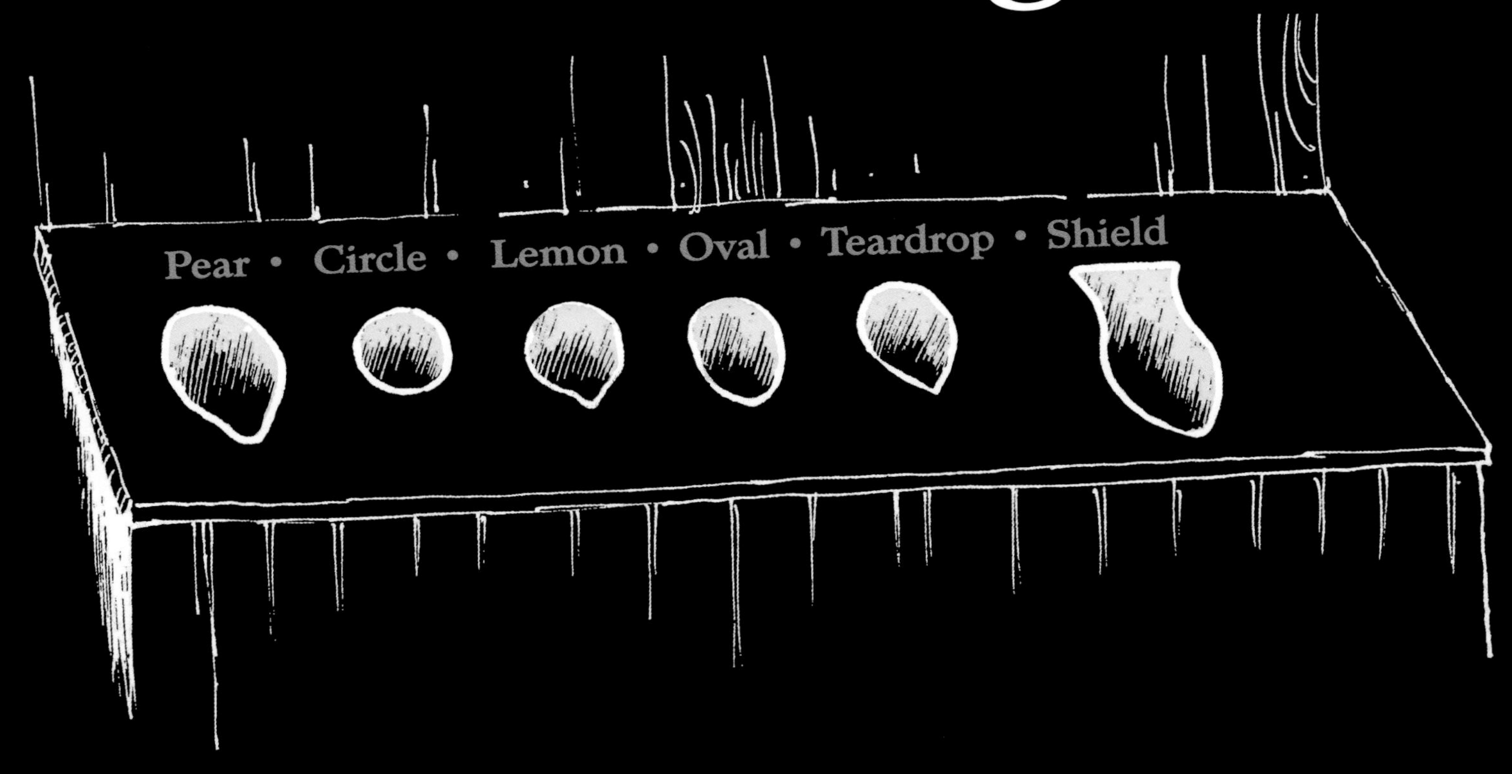

Much can be said about privy holes and why there were so many designs. Certainly most were intended to be comfortable, and common logic dictates ones with smooth, flowing curved lines gave the user the most comfort. After the hole was cut into the seatboard, it was rounded and smoothed to give an inward cavosurface bevel. Square holes with 90 degree line angles were nonexistent along the White Oak. In some regions of the nation, diamond holes (almost a square hole rotated 90°) did exist.

In some communities along the White Oak, the same hole design was repetitive. It could have been because the same builder built numerous outhouses with the same design characteristics, or probably neighbors simply copied another neighbor's design.

If one hole were noticeably smaller, it was usually designed for the children and was known as the "kiddy–hole". In some outhouses, even the adult holes were made markedly small so that odor could be contained or suppressed with a cap over the hole when it was not in use.

Circles were more suitable for the short, round, dainty users; long-legged, slender people fitted well to an oval or teardrop design; larger holes like the shield were for broad–beamed, slab–bottomed types.

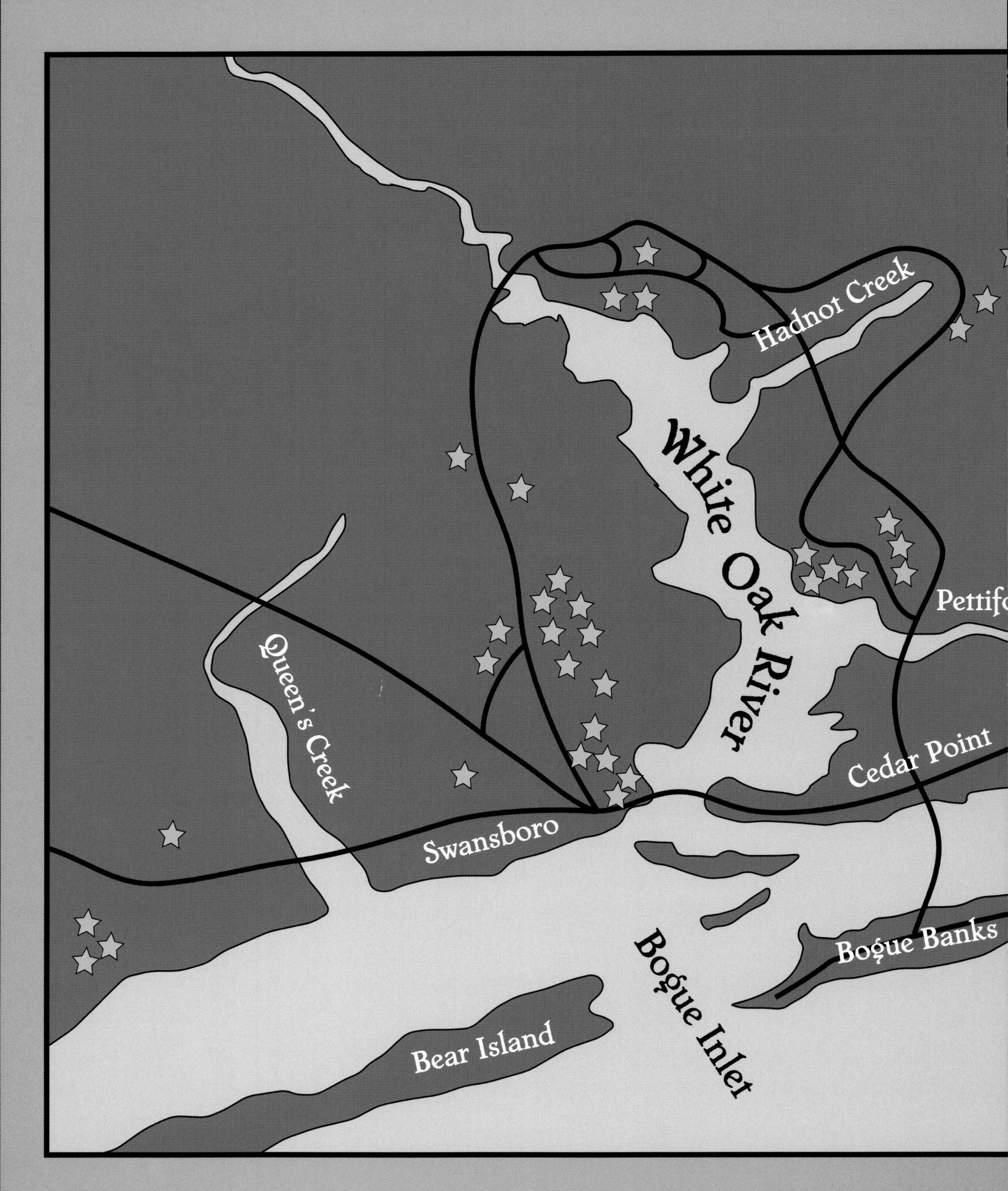

Outhouses along the White Oak River

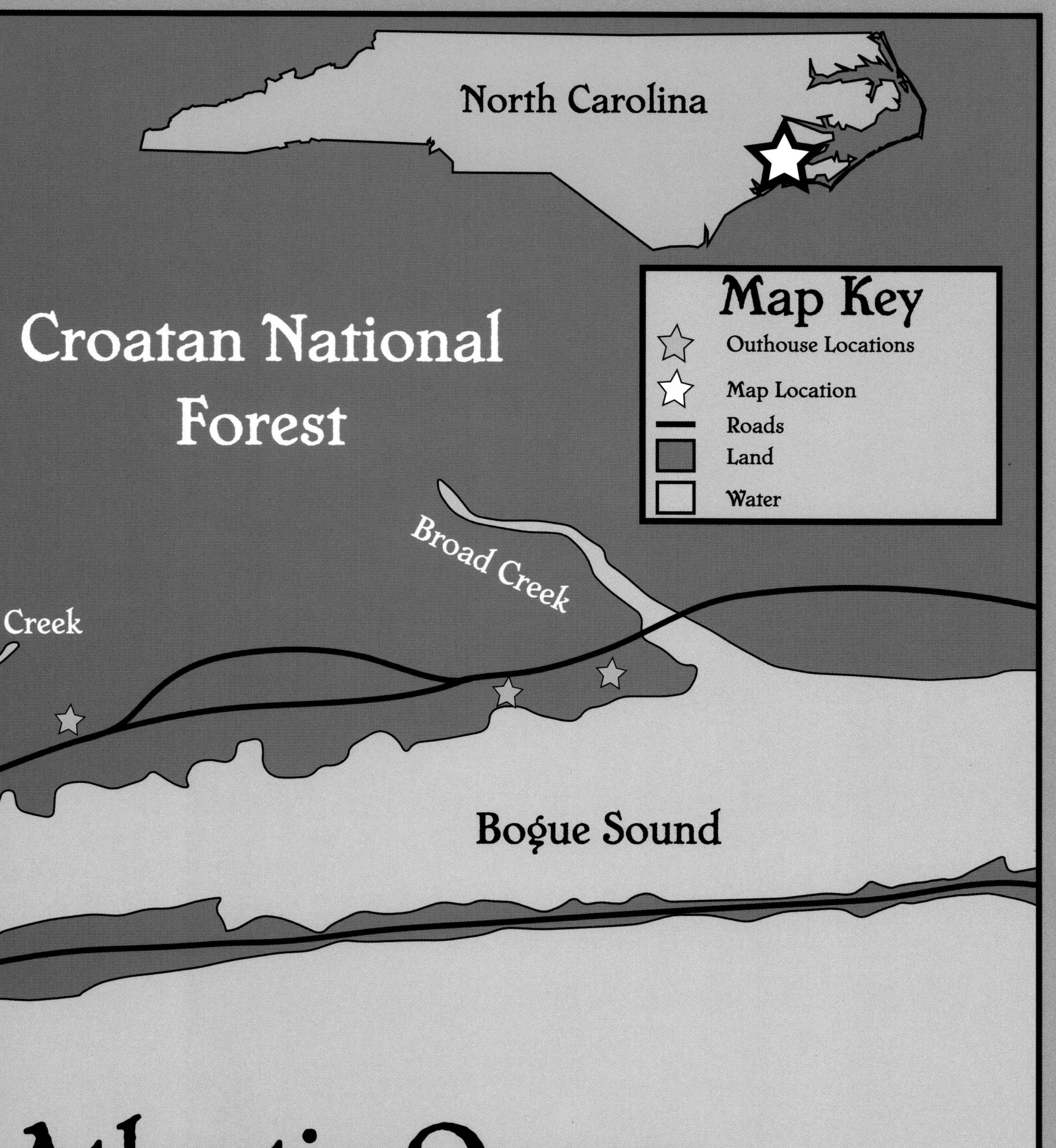

and adjoining communities in 1976.

A classic lean–to with a moon painted on in later years as a joke. Note the small knob for outside closure. When the occupant was inside, the door was closed and fastened usually by a metal hook. On northern outhouses the door opened inward because snow drifts would prevent it swinging outward

Note this outhouse, as well as the one on the preceding page, was built on a concrete slab. These were later models or Depression era types. Note the doors swing outward, never inward on outhouses along the White Oak river.

A room with a view.

A nice pair of pear-shaped holes. Outhouses were simple, functional and built to serve a basic human need. There was no place for modesty in the old days. The most delicate sounds could be heard even on windy days.

(above & right)
Two examples of painted, well maintained outhouses that later served as tool sheds. Few outhouses were painted, most were left unpainted and aged naturally. Note the triangular vent was partially closed in the above outhouse.

This outhouse was one of only two remaining in Swansboro in 1976. Its final years were spent holding the end of a clothesline. Even though it was well maintained, its demise was inevitable. The architectural design was its death knell. Everyone knew what the classic lean–to signified, and in later years outhouses, even the well maintained ones, were a source of embarrassment.

The only outhouse still standing in the Swansboro city limits, a pitched–roof or vault–ed–ceiling design. It has survived only because of its fine architectural characteristics. Had it been a lean–to, it would have been demolished. Many people think the building served as the Swansboro Post Office during the early part of the century. Not so...after being decommissioned as an outhouse, it has been maintained as a tool shed and storage building.

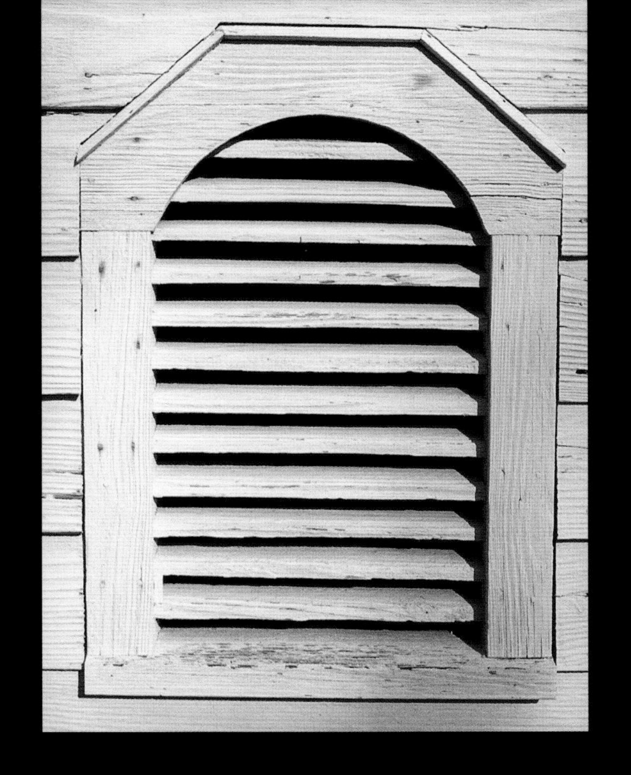

The rear view showing the fancy louvered or slat vent.

An interior picture of a North Carolina privy license. There was an era when privies had to be inspected, and most had a cardboard license of approval stapled in the interior. No doubt, many were never inspected.

Splendor in the tall grass.

(Above) A striking, vaulted-ceiling outhouse with clapboard siding. The thick, viny growth has preserved this structure for many years.

Ask and you shall learn; seek and you shall find.

(Below) Interior view of the above outhouse, good seats still available. A well crafted one-seater, three-holer with hole covers. No smoking. Leave your butt outside! The foul odor from deep down is merely methane gas laced with noxious, odorous bacteria, and is highly flammable and combustible. The toilet holes served as portals for natural gas going down and natural gas rising up. Smoking in an outhouse could be very dangerous. This could be an uplifting experience. Note the charred back wall. Young boys caused a fire when smoking. It is amusing that people seek refuge or privacy in a toilet for reasons other than making a call to nature.

From the past. The nation's most recognized piece of outhouse literature.

Passing of the Backhouse

When memory keeps me company
and moves to smiles or tears,
A weather-beaten object looms
through the mist of years.
Behind the house and barn it stood,
a hundred yards or more,
And hurrying feet a path had made,
straight for its swinging door.

Its architecture was a form
of simple classic art,
But in the tragedy of life
it played a leading part.
And oft the passing traveler
drove slow, and heaved a sign,
To see the modest hired girl
slip out with glances shy.

We had our poesy garden
that the women loved so well,
I loved it too, but better still
I loved the stronger smell
That filled the evening breezes
so full of homely cheer,
And told the night-o'ertaken tramp
that human life was near.

On lazy August afternoons,
it made a little bower,
Delightful, where my grandsire sat
and whiled away an hour.
For there the morning-glory
its very eaves entwined,
And berry bushes reddened
in the steaming soil behind.

All day fat spiders spun their webs
to catch the buzzing flies
That flitted to and from the house,
where Ma was baking pies.
And once a swarm of hornets bold,
had built a palace there,
And stung my unsuspecting aunt –
I must not tell you where.

Then Father took a flaming pole –
that was a happy day –
He nearly burned the building up,
but the hornets left to stay.
When summer blooms began to fade
and winter to carouse
We banked the little buildings with
a heap of hemlock boughs.

But when the crust was on the snow
and the sullen skies were gray
In sooth the building was no place
where one would wish to stay.
We did our duties promptly,
there one purpose swayed the mind;
We tarried not, nor lingered long
on what we left behind.

The torture of that icy seat
would make a Spartan sob,
For needs must scrape the goose flesh
with a lacerating cob,
That from a frost-encrusted nail,,
was suspended by a string
My Father was a frugal man
and wasted not a thing.

When grandpa had to "go out back"
and make his morning call
We'd bundle up the dear old man
with a muffler and a shawl,
I knew the hole on which he sat –
'twas padded all around,
And once I dared to sit there –
'twas all too wide I found.

My loins were all too little,
and I jackknifed there to stay,
They had to come and cut me out,
or I'd have passed away.
Then father said ambition
was a thing that a boys should shun,
And I must use the children's hole
'till childhood days were done.

And still I marvel at the craft
that cut those holes so true.
The baby hole, and slender hole
that fitted Sister Sue.
That dear old country landmark;
I've tramped around a bit,
And in the lap of luxury
my lot has been to sit,

But ere I die I'll eat the fruit
of trees I've robbed of yore,
Then seek the shanty where my name
is carved upon the door.
I ween the old familiar smell
will sooth my jaded soul,
I'm now a man but non the less,
I'll try the children's hole.

— James Whitcomb Riley

The poem has also been attributed to Eugene Smith.

Making tracks out back.
You never know what it is to have to go

House of meditation at the White Oak Unitarian Church and interior view of the box seat. Some seats were painted white to make them more visible at dusk. In later years, people updated handhewn seats with commercially made commode seats for additional comfort.

From the past.

The W. C.

There was a little old lady school teacher looking for a room in the country. She asked the local school master to help her. A place that suited her was found, and she returned to the city for her luggage. She remembered that she had not noticed a bathroom, or, as she called it, a water closet. She wrote the school master and asked whether or not there was a W. C. in or near the house.

The school master, who did not know the expression, was puzzled by the W. C., never dreaming that she was talking about a bathroom. He finally sought the advice of the local minister. They decided that W. C. must mean Wayside Chapel. The lady received the following letter a few days later:

Dear Madam,

The W. C. is located nine miles from the house in the heart of a beautiful grove of trees. It will seat 350 people at one time, and it is open on Tuesday, Thursday and Sunday of each week. Some people like to take their lunch and make a day of it. Thursday there is organ accompaniment. The acoustics are very good, and the slightest sound can be heard by everyone. It may interest you to know that my daughter met her husband at the W. C. We are now in the process of taking donations to purchase plush seats. We feel this is a long felt need, since the present seats have holes in them. My wife is rather delicate; therefore she hasn't been able to attend regularly. It has been six months since she last went. Naturally it pains her very much not to go more often.

I will close with the desire to accommodate you in every possible way and will be happy to save you a seat down near the front door, whichever you prefer.

A well preserved lean–to with the door still intact. Note the drip cap above the roof.

(Above) A well constructed lean–to with a columnar vent and drip cap over the door. Also note the door knob. (Bringing in the age of porcelain) (Left) Interior view showing the columnar vent and trap door hole cover. The interior has been painted, a rarity for rural outhouses. The owner was very fastidious, and cleanliness was next to Godliness. (Right) Privy plans provided by the North Carolina State Board of Health.

From the past

If nature bid you here to come to do the duty that must be done, be neat and clean, and one thing more, put down the lid and shut the door.

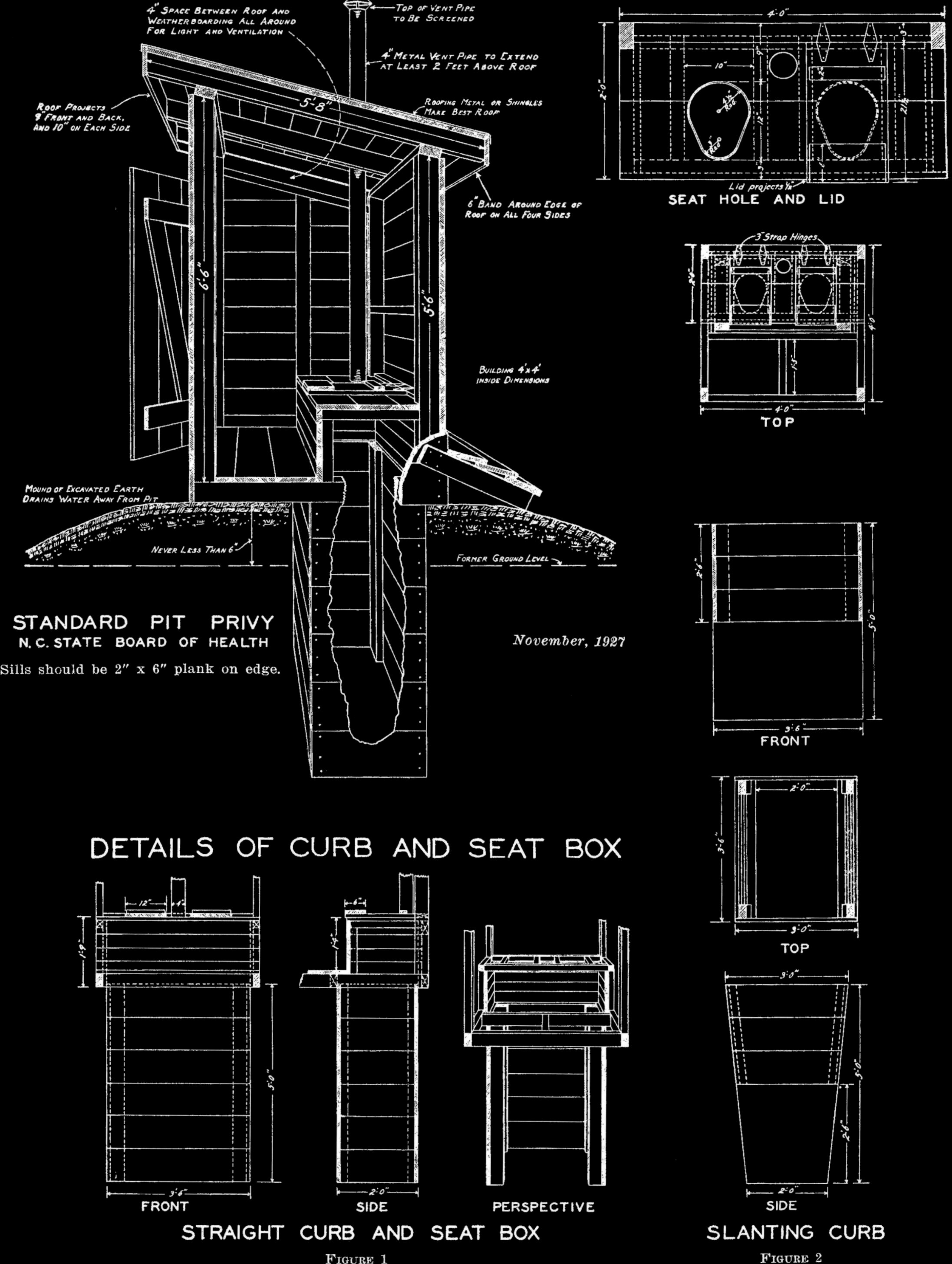

Figure 1

Figure 2

An over–water outhouse in the background of an early 1900s picture of the Swansboro waterfront. Note three men loitering next to the outhouse. Today we look back and find the practice of using an over–water facility appalling, yet people of all civilizations and nationalities have historically used their rivers and lakes for sewers. Even as late as the 1950s, raw sewage was deposited into the White Oak River, and it was not an uncommon sight to be out swimming and see a "Baby Ruth" floating by.

(Above) Note the barely discernible over-water lean-to with the conspicuous square vent (gun port). Beware of snapping turtles on high tide! (Below) The same outhouse on Water Street after Hurricane Hazel, 1954. This outhouse was a one-holer with an oval hole, and the bench seat was painted white.

A tin–type lean–to with a wooden door. Note the overhang-
ing piece of tin that has served as a drip cap and how well
the door has been preserved.

Chickens around outhouses caused many problems, particularly with surface privies. They would not only pick through the droppings and spread disease but would also nest in corners beneath the seat. Occasionally, one would enter the toilet through one of the seat holes and make a nest inside. As I walked up to examine the interior, the chicken (left) raced me to the door... sorry folks, this seat's taken!

A classic lean–to, tin–type with inefficient venting. The advantage in using tin is that the door does not warp. One advantage of the lean–to design, as noted by outhouse humorist Chic Sale, the door can be extended to the top of the structure, and no matter how wide the door is opened, it never bumps into the roof.

A “high rise” pit privy built in the 1970s. In yesteryear, surface privies built on the side of hills or embankments were known as “long drop” privies.

A lean-to with a commercially made made toilet. There were many types of factory made toilets, especially in Europe. Most noted of all sanitary engineer designers was Thomas Crapper. His name lives on. Even after some old timers acquired indoor plumbing, a few still preferred to go outdoors. The typical comment was, "I'll go out where I have plenty of room." Old habits are hard to break.

the slop jar. It had a lid and was hidden beneath the bed or in the corner of a closet and was brought out when needed. Emptying the slop jar or pee pot was a chore for the next morning. The containers were washed thoroughly and left out in the sun to dry. In more urbanized areas and in the North, people used an all porcelain piece of stoneware known as the thundermug.

Passing of the Thundermug

Some sing of spring and its infinite charms
Of brooks and green meadows, of cities and farms.
Some chant of the lily, the lilac and the rose
And love in the height of its sweetest repose.
There are rhymes to the dust of a quaint village street,
And the subjects galore that I need not repeat,
But little, O little, has ever been said
Of the old fashion thundermug under the bed.
The title oft varied as you will recall,
By which it was known to one and to all
To some it was known as chamber y'see
The men called it pot, and the children called it "pottee"
I've heard it referred to because of its stench,
As the odiferous "left handed monkey wrench."
Women said vessel and would blush crimson red
At the mention of thundermug under the bed.

Newt Hopkins

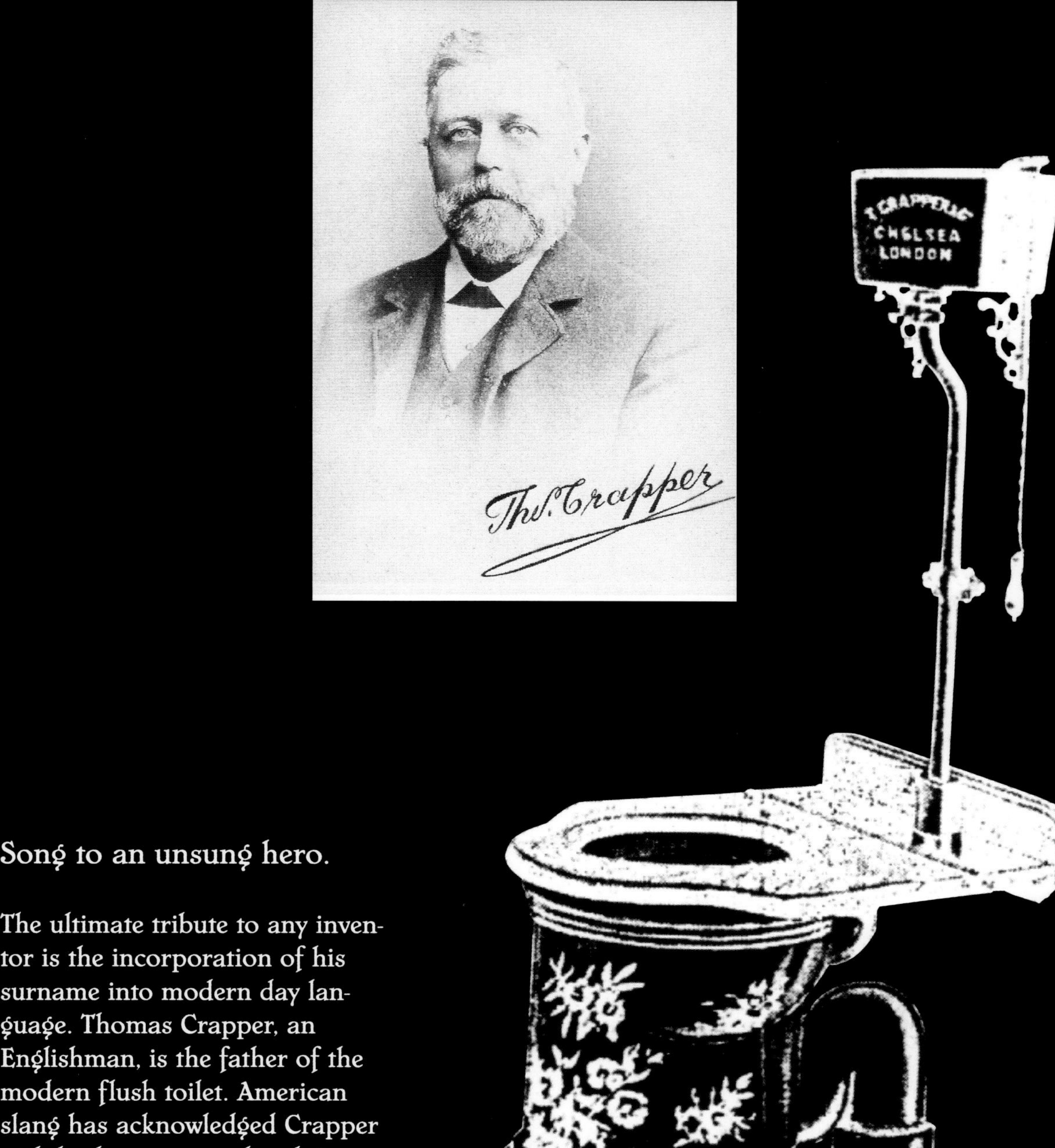

Song to an unsung hero.

The ultimate tribute to any inventor is the incorporation of his surname into modern day language. Thomas Crapper, an Englishman, is the father of the modern flush toilet. American slang has acknowledged Crapper with both a noun and verb in a dubious sort of fame. Sir John Harrington invented the first indoor flush toilet, but it was Thomas Crapper who invented valveless, water conserving toilet.
In the 1870s, the British Board Of Trade sent out a call for a more efficient flushing system on toilets, and Crapper, a Chelsea sanitary engineer, came up with the best solution. His ingenious design, which can still be seen beneath the lid of toilet tanks, depends on a float, a metal arm and a siphon action to empty a reservoir behind the toilet bowl. A book has been written as a special tribute to him. The title is **Flushed With Pride: The Story of Thomas Crapper.**

Some outhouses were tucked behind other buildings to give timid or modest ladies a little more privacy.

From the Past.

An old timer named the behind–the–barn style the "twilet". His wife was very modest and did not want anyone to know when she had to go. When she went out to use the toilet it was usually about sundown, and she would say that she was going out to catch the twilight. (Twilight + toilet = "twilet".)

Having the outhouse near the woodpile or smokehouse was also face saving for the modest ladies. If they were going out to use the toilet and men were around, they could change their minds and bring a few sticks of wood or a piece of meat back to the house. Note the outhouse and smokehouse in the background. Also note the cedar shakes on the dwelling, the wooden gutter and rain barrel for catching drinking water.

A picturesque "twilet" in a bucolic, setting. The aged, rustic siding matches the planking on the barn. The beauty of aged wood is one of time's masterpieces.

The location of the outhouse was always behind the dwelling, usually at the far corner of the lot. This kept the stench and insects away from the home and gave the user a little distance. As mentioned earlier, "twilets" were tucked behind other buildings. Summer folks obtained privacy by planting wisteria or morning glory on lattice-work in front of the outhouse. Shady, secluded spots were favored. Users preferred a cool place in the summer, and some preferred privacy in all seasons.

(Far left) An aged lean–to, almost concealed by years of overgrowth. The door should have had a pair of twining hearts as a cut out. The vintage photograph is a picture of newlyweds shortly after marriage. They always went together. Back then, there was almost no divorce. Now virtually everyone has his or her private bathroom in a nice home, and divorce is rampant. The couples who went together stayed together.

"Togetherness" holes. The lidded holes were loves gilded links for the above couple. The names of this devoted couple have been withheld in order to protect their scatological innocence.

A doorless dooley. Rural institutions like wooden schools and churches had privacy partitions rather than doors. This design was also known as the foyer style.

The owner of this outhouse did not need a door, for he lived an isolated life in a remote area along the White Oak River. The outbuilding on the left served as a privacy barrier.

From the past.

Both cut outs and windows are European architectural designs going back to the days of early castles. The window was "wind–eye" or "wind–o", an opening for both the wind and eye. The wind blows in, and the eye looks out.

Segregated facilities. A pair of outhouses, one for the men and one for the women. (Right) A close up view of one of the vents in the men's facility, a diamond in the rough.

A four-holer, double-headed dooley. One side for the men, one for the women. This outhouse is of World War II vintage and was located on Bogue Air Field. Military men have traditionally called a toilet the head.

From the past.

Back in the 50s, a northern city slicker was passing through North Carolina on his way to Florida and stopped at a country store to buy gas and use the necessary facilities. The facility was a three-holer behind the store. He entered, sat down and began to relieve himself. About that time, an old farmer entered, pulled down the strap on his bib overalls and bent over to take a seat. At the same time, a nickel and two pennies rolled out of his pants pocket into the middle hole. All of a sudden the farmer jumped up, whipped out his billfold, rolled up a twenty dollar bill and sailed it down the middle hole. The city slicker said, "What did you do that for!" Said the old farmer, "You didn't think I was going down there for a nickel and two pennies, did you?"

A lean–to precariously leaning into its shadow. Hurry sundown. Getting too old to stand alone, but still resisting the pull of gravity.

It is symbolic that lean–tos are also called "leanders." It is always tempting to give the tired, aging structure a final shove, but an outhouse preservationist never does. Outhouses have traditionally been a part of Halloween pranks throughout the country. Pranksters have uprooted them and placed them in all sorts of places on Halloween night

(Above) Looking down Breezy Point Road, 1976. (Below) Same view in 1946. Note the "comfort sta
tion" or "country telephone booth" on the left side of the road. I mentioned to an older resident i
the community about seeing the outhouse in an old picture of the road. I assumed it had vanishec
with time, but the old man said it was still there.

(Above) Close up of the outhouse on Breezy Point Road. It was covered with many years of tangled growth, but is discernible upon close examination. (Below) The outhouse has been "hulled out" or cleared of vegetation. Note the size as compared to other lean-tos. It is much larger than the classic one- or two-holer.

ouse on the preceding pages. Multi–holers
dn' house" style or "togetherness" holes. We
a congenial place to meet. This three–holer
time. The wood has acquired a beautiful
produce. What may appear as crude to
nost romantic, appeal to others. This is
nest -- a functional, utilitarian object now

To enter vintage outhouses today g
for inner reverie. The outhouses br
and carefree years. They remind u
dark, dank down under. We can vi
noses and straining with a grunt. I
out was one of life's elemental plea
cool breezes blowing through the v
days when life was simple.

Hadnot Creek Primitive Baptist Church lean–to in shambles and almost toppled over. Outhouses have also been dubbed "temples of convenience," a place where one could make an offering to Mother Earth.

(Below) Interior view of the outhouse. A two–holer with the seat on the right being a "kiddy hole," one designed for the children. Despite being abandoned and shut off from the outside world, rays of sunlight beamed through cracks in the walls.

From the past

Thou shalt have a place also with out the camp, whither thou shalt go forth abroad: And thou shalt have a paddle upon thy weapon; and it shall be, when thou wilt ease thyself abroad, thou shalt dig therewith, and shalt turn back and cover that which cometh from thee:
Deuteronomy 23: 12 13.

Gone with the wind.

(Left) A lean–to shrouded by nature's greenery.
(Above) A flat–top slowly being claimed by Mother Nature.

(Left) An outhouse with two knobs or buttons. Note a reinforcing plank or batten has been nailed to the top of the door to correct the warping problem. (Below) Interior picture of the outhouse. No job's finished 'till the paperwork is done.

A country lady making a symbolic presentation of the evolution of the corn cob era to the rolled, toilet tissue era. What significant era has she omitted?

Interior of the outhouse on Page 73. Note the mellowed corn cobs and the dingy Sears & Roebuck catalog. My great uncle was a frugal man who never threw away anything. I thought the use of corn cobs was always a joke...not so. The use of corn cobs in the early 1900s was quite pervasive. James Whitcomb Riley described the corncob as lacerating. Now we know the origin of the expression "rough as a cob". If there were a choice, as shown above, it was proper etiquette for the men to use the corn cobs, and the catalog pages were saved for the ladies.

The art and science of using different color corn cobs... ask a friend.

From the past

The corn cob was the most sanitary instrument nature ever devised for the use to which it was devoted by our ancestors, and human invention has not improved upon it. Nobody's finger ever slipped through a corn cob, and the corn cob was non skidding. – W. O. Saunders, **The Independent**, 1934... Elizabeth City, N.C.

(Left) A tin–type flat–top. As mentioned earlier, flat–tops were ill conceived designs, for most flat–tops inevitably leaked. Many of the outhouse doors had not been opened in decades, and it gives one an uneasy, eerie surge of adrenaline to tug a door open that has been closed so long. There is always the thought of hornets, wasps, bats and even of snakes waiting to make a strike. (Below) A tear drop shaped hole. I named this one the "screamer," for it reminds me of looking down a throat with no tonsils. Of all the holes and outhouses along the White Oak, this was my favorite.